IMAGES
of America

BEACH HAVEN

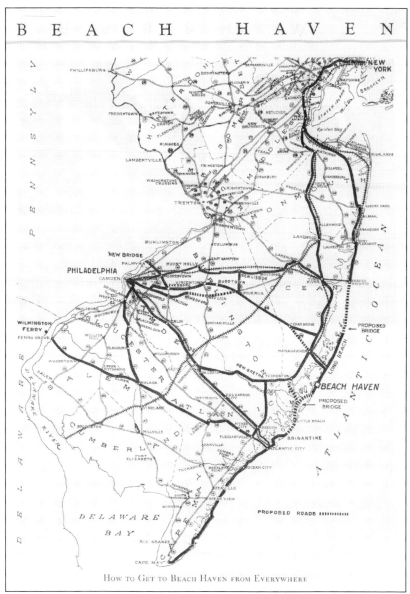

How to Get to Beach Haven from Everywhere

Before 1886, access to the barrier island of Long Beach was by sailboat or steam yacht only. Visitors left from mainland towns such as Tuckerton, Manahawkin, or Barnegat. In 1885, the Tuckerton Railroad expanded its route from Manahawkin to Long Beach Island. Soon, there were spurs south to Beach Haven and north to Barnegat City. The popular summer excursion routes from Philadelphia and New York to the New Jersey shore are highlighted in this map. (Collection of the New Jersey Maritime Museum.)

ON THE COVER: Dock Road led from the public wharf to one block west of the center of town on Bay Avenue. Supplies and building materials originally arrived by sailboat, as did visitors and residents of Beach Haven. Dock Road was a corduroy road, made of logs covered by sand and gravel. Only sneakboxes and rowing skiffs could navigate the adjoining Mud Hen Creek. Across the marshes, the large oceanfront Hotel Baldwin can be seen along with the wooden water tower and early residences. (Collection of the New Jersey Maritime Museum.)

IMAGES
of America

BEACH HAVEN

Gretchen F. Coyle and
Deborah C. Whitcraft

ARCADIA
PUBLISHING

Published by Arcadia Publishing
Charleston, South Carolina

Printed in the United States of America

Library of Congress Control Number: 2018930634

For all general information, please contact Arcadia Publishing:
Telephone 843-853-2070
Fax 843-853-0044
E-mail sales@arcadiapublishing.com
For customer service and orders:
Toll-Free 1-888-313-2665

Visit us on the Internet at www.arcadiapublishing.com

*This book is dedicated to all who are drawn to the
beauty, mystique, and history of Beach Haven.*

CONTENTS

ACKNOWLEDGMENTS

An original black leather–bound book, *Views of Beach Haven: Beach Haven Realty, Beach Haven*, was donated to the New Jersey Maritime Museum (NJMM) by trustee Robert Cunningham. In this book, Beach Haven is proclaimed "the greatest opportunity at the seashore." This late-1800s prospectus or image book was designed to lure investors to the new town. Most of the photographs are thought to have been taken by Robert Fry Engle.

A 2015 call to the NJMM from antique dealer James Dunn, of Green Valley, Arizona, led to the acquisition, by NJMM trustee George Hartnett, of a scrapbook of Robert Fry Engle's original photographs. These photographs take us back over a century; readers will see the development of a newly formed town called Beach Haven—almost called Beach Heaven—by founder Archelaus Pharo's daughter, who declared the area to be "heaven."

The photographs in this book are from the collection of the New Jersey Maritime Museum. Unlike artists, photographers do not always sign their work, yet they did their own developing, experimenting with processes such as albumen, silver, and platinum prints. Panoramic scenes were popular in the late 1800s, giving historians views of the southern end of an unspoiled barrier island.

Robert Fry Engle spent his younger days as a professional photographer under the tutelage of famous photographer Burton Holmes. When Robert Barclay Engle became ill in the 1890s, he summoned his son to help run his hotel, the Engleside, in Beach Haven. Fortunately for all who appreciate our area's history, Robert Fry Engle continued his pursuit of photographic subjects, capturing the beauty of Beach Haven in a bygone era.

We wish to express our sincere appreciation to Jeanette Lloyd, Beach Haven's historian and president of the Beach Haven Historic Preservation Advisory Commission, for her assistance. Her unparalleled knowledge of Beach Haven's history and the people who played an important role in its development is legend. Without her dedication and demand for accuracy, this book would not have been possible.

All proceeds from sales of this book support the mission of the New Jersey Maritime Museum.

INTRODUCTION

There have been more visitors to Beach Haven this season than ever at the resort. The season began early in June, July was a great month, and August has witnessed crowds that have taxed the resort.

Beach Haven . . . has great natural beauty, is free from land breezes and offers every opportunity for a genuine good time.

—Beach Haven Realty News, 1913

Since the town of Beach Haven was founded in 1874 and incorporated in 1890, large "cottages" had been built, railroad usage to Long Beach Island with spurs north and south was growing, and an "automobile highway" was under construction. An automobile parade was planned for June 1914 when a new causeway would be completed.

A "great new city" was advertised in the *Beach Haven Realty News*. Investment opportunities seemed limitless:

The development is of the highest character – there is no skimping in anything. The men who are back of the Company have many thousands of dollars invested in Beach Haven in private enterprises, aside from their holdings in the Company, and they realize the necessity of doing things right.

Those who buy land in Beach Haven now are making an investment that will return large profits. Enhancement of values goes on with every bit of development—every house that is erected adds to the value of the surrounding land.

An enthusiasm pervaded the air around Beach Haven. Early pioneers and their families had been moving across Little Egg Harbor Bay from places like New Gretna, Tuckerton, and Parkertown. The men earned money as seasonal boat captains—their pride and expertise resulting in the formation of the Beach Haven Yacht Club. The town was dubbed the "Fishing Capital of the World." In addition, there were clammers, oystermen, hunting and fishing guides with unparalleled knowledge of local waters. Wives worked in the hotels, took in laundry and sewing, and were teachers and community leaders. The early residents were determined to earn enough money to last through the cold winters.

The Beach Haven Realty Company, located in the Crozer Building in Philadelphia, set its sights on the wealthy from Philadelphia, the Main Line, and Burlington County. They wanted to sell lots for summer homes and recoup a percentage of their investment by building both large Victorians and smaller bungalows. One Beach Haven Realty ad summed up Beach Haven as "a good place with which to get acquainted."

Charles Beck had coined the phrase "An Island Six Miles at Sea. No Land Breezes. Today's Best Seashore Real Estate Investment Opportunity." (The island is not quite six miles from the mainland—actually closer to four—but Beck's phrase had a special ring to it.) Investors in the new town of Beach Haven were intertwined, owning interests in the Beach Haven Construction Company, Ostendorf's Garage, and the Beach Haven Building and Loan Association. In addition, they had financial interests in the developments of Sea Haven and St. Albans on Tucker's Island.

Beauty was seen everywhere in spite of a flat, barren, sandy terrain occasionally washed over by ocean or bay. There were no fancy gardens or parks. Any natural sand dunes were cut back for ocean views. Sand blew off the beach creating sand-covered gravel roads. Dune grasses popped up in spots; beach peas and rugosa roses provided color along with the white spring blossoms of beach plums and tall yuccas. Large rose mallow flowers grew wild; homeowners planted hydrangeas, providing splashes of pink, purple, and blue, which did not need any maintenance. Wild cranberries and blueberries were found in the sand.

Bayberry provided greenery, along with scented candles made from the gray berries in midsummer. The scent of honeysuckle filled the air on windless summer evenings. Large prickly pear cactus blossoms yielded bright yellow flowers protruding from annoying spines. Fall brought shoots of goldenrod. Near the bay were marsh grasses, hosts to flies and mosquitoes every summer.

Hunting along the New Jersey shore was referred to as "gunning." Before 1917, there were no rules for hunting. Men who participated in this popular sport could shoot as much as they liked. After their guides or families cooked a bit of their kill, the rest were handed out to local people who were pleased to have a good bird to cook.

In a time before hunting restrictions, birds of all types flew overhead along the Atlantic Flyway. Terns, gulls, and herons were part of the everyday scenery. Ducks, geese, and shorebirds were fair game for hunters who came to "gun" in Beach Haven, venturing off in hunting parties or with savvy guides. Many dinners consisted of roasted wild birds surrounded with fresh, local vegetables from backyard gardens that had been mulched with eel grass and fish guts. Shorebird pot pie was a favorite, using bite-sized breasts baked in gravy and pastry.

Luckily for all of us, a great interest in photography was developing. The start and growth of Beach Haven's formative years were chronicled. There were photographers located in Beach Haven's two big hotels, the Baldwin and the Engleside. A Mr. Roper had a small shop in the Engleside Hotel. Some of his photographs were made into popular postcards. Louis P. Seldon's store was located on the boardwalk, overlooking the ocean. He advertised, "Kodak films developed, prices right, work right."

Both amateur and professional photographers managed to capture the emerging town of Beach Haven from unusual places. There are pictures taken from the top floors and towers of the Engleside and Baldwin hotels, as well as the water tower. Panoramic shots featured unique bay and ocean scenes.

Without a doubt, the most talented photographer was Robert Fry Engle, who took over the Engleside Hotel from his father Robert Barclay Engle. The elder Engle managed the Parry House (which burned down in 1881) for a few years. With ideas for a very large and fancy hotel, he built the Engleside in 1876 with the financial help of his cousin Samuel Engle.

The younger Engle always wanted to be a photographer and had no interest in property management. However, when his father died on May 15, 1901, in Mount Holly, New Jersey, Robert Fry Engle's vocation was determined. Fortunately, he left his avocation of photography as our heritage.

Charles Beck's magnificent home, which he simply referred to as "the Farm," stood alone surrounded by lawn and gardens. Liberty Thorofare, Mordecai Island, and Little Egg Harbor Bay were to the west of the home. Striped awnings and open windows provided a bit of shade and cool air. An orchestra occasionally played in the enclosed south parlor—gentlemen in coats and ties with a conductor leading the group. Fall photographs showed contented hunters at the farm—usually Charles Beck's influential friends.

Families are seen on the beach in wool bathing suits enjoying the sand and fresh air and dipping into the Atlantic. The popularity of fishing continued to draw visitors who came to hire proud charter boat captains who dressed the part in wool jackets, ties, and captains' hats. They were well spoken and extremely knowledgeable, providing bait, reels ,and a sense of where the best fish could be caught. The Beach Haven Yacht Club was formed for the charter boat fishermen who drew ample crowds during the summer months. In the early 1920s, masts were cut off the sailboats, and motors were installed for faster access to the fishing grounds. New wooden powerboats were built.

Homes in various states of construction were a fascination for photographers, showing building techniques and small details such as wooden barrels of nails. As a sign of the times, some construction workers were formally dressed in jackets and ties. It is unfathomable to think that the first homes were built with wood washed up on the beach or brought from the mainland on sailboats along with all other supplies.

Homes on Ocean Street and Berkeley Avenues were built close to the sandy streets. Only a few hedges or low fences delineated property lines. All had porches where families gathered to relax and catch the breeze. Artesian wells provided fresh water. The Engleside and Baldwin Hotels advertised running salt water in addition to fresh water in their bathrooms. Visitors, however, changed in bathhouses in front of the hotels abutting the boardwalk and close to the beaches. Sandy, wet wool bathing suits were not allowed in the hotels.

Strollers walked the small, low oceanside boardwalk hoping to see and be seen, much as people do today at Beach Haven's bayside attractions. Children gravitate to the sand and ocean. On a normal day, one could see a hundred or more large vessels offshore.

The original 1904 St. Thomas Aquinas Roman Catholic Church on Fourth Street and Beach Avenue was built at a cost of $4,000. During the summer, the door stood open with windows propped outward. The first pastor resided at the Baldwin Hotel during the season. A bell hung in the belfry. The church stood virtually by itself, except for three houses visible on Third Street.

In 1885, the Tuckerton & Long Beach Railroad was established through marshy islands and over Manahawkin Bay to the island once simply called Long Beach. It was a huge improvement over being at the mercy of wind and weather in a boat. A single track went north to Barnegat City and south to Beach Haven. Visitors opened the train windows to breathe in the smell of pungent marshes and briny ocean, much as they do today with a touch of a button while driving over the causeway.

Ostendorf's Garage loomed huge in Beach Haven when it was built for automobiles in the early 1900s. (The first cars were brought to the island by barge.) White-walled tires gleamed; chauffeurs in distinctive caps were proud of the cars they drove around Beach Haven. A small wooden sign simply stated Beach Haven Garage on the front of the large two-story brick edifice.

In 1914, the Automobile Causeway was opened with a parade and celebration. Mobility had come to Beach Haven. Cars could be driven through the dusty Pine Barrens and over to the island, thrilling car lovers. Bunting decorated homes in Beach Haven.

Gaff-rigged, wide, wooden sailboats were used in the bay for transportation, fishing, excursions, and eventually racing. Over a hundred years later, catboats are still raced in many locations along the bays of Barnegat and Little Egg Harbor. Robert Fry Engle found beauty in photographing whatever was going on. Through his hobby, a history of the town of Beach Haven was recorded from many heights and numerous angles showing clouds, sparkling water, sails full of wind, and children making magic on the beach.

Photographs in this book portray the raw beauty of early Beach Haven before and after development. The town is seen as a place like no other, surrounded on two sides by water, where families could partake of the new concept of leisure time, visit with family and friends, and leave responsibilities and business on the mainland.

One

A TOWN BUILT ON SAND

Beach Haven, New Jersey

The lure of the ocean and the beach would have been enough to get many summer visitors to Beach Haven. After all, who is not captivated by fresh air, cool breezes, and relaxation on the beach? A number of influential and intelligent businessmen worked together to literally build a town in the sand. With a lot of financial backers and New Jersey politicians working together, Beach Haven declared itself to be the Queen City.

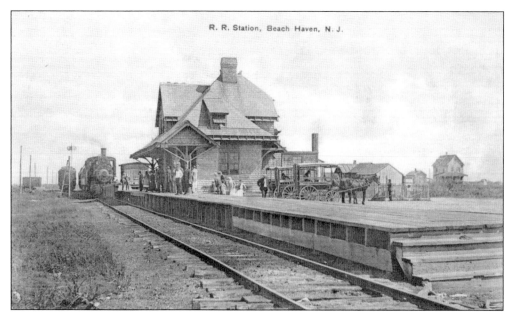

Owned by parent company Pennsylvania Railroad, the Beach Haven Railroad Station was built in 1886. This early photograph shows wagons and horses. It was a substantial building with an area for purchasing tickets and a waiting room. Located on Third Street, a block west of Bay Avenue, it originally stood in the marshes. In 1900, the round-trip fare from Camden to Beach Haven was $2.

Rapid Transit at Beach Haven, N. J.

Who would not have felt special being met at the Beach Haven Station by a striped canopied train car pulled on a track by a horse? While the Engleside and the Hotel Baldwin appeared to support each other's endeavors, there was fierce competition underneath. When the horsecars from the station took guests to the Baldwin, they passed the Engleside. This made the Engleside management furious, and they sued to keep the striped canopy tram off of Atlantic Avenue.

Was this a special day at the Beach Haven train station? Ladies are stylishly dressed in long white cotton and linen dresses and a few in black. As train usage slowed down and finally ended around 1935, the train station was privately owned by a series of individuals. Finally, around 1993, the building was too far gone for anyone to care about. The property was sold and a new home was built.

Over the "plains" to Beach Haven, N. J.

It was a hard drive through the Pine Barrens to the shore. From cities like Philadelphia and New York, ferries were taken across water to get to New Jersey. These tedious, dusty roads had to be traveled slowly to prevent flat tires or overheated engines. The few restaurants along the way were still referred to as stagecoach stops. What is now a two-hour trip could take a full day.

BEACH HAVEN, N. J.   Two-Mile Automobile Bridge over Little Egg Harbor Bay.

The bridge across Manahawkin Bay (mistakenly cited here as Little Egg Harbor Bay) was a "two mile automobile bridge." Made of wood, it made ceaseless clip-clop sounds as the tires rolled across the wood. In addition, seagulls dropped clamshells on the bridge, so the noise was even louder at times. Metal railings prevented accidents on each side of the bridge.

Rapid Transit in Beach Haven.   Published by A. J. Durand.

Many stayed for the summer, or at least a few weeks. This J. Durand postcard shows the Baldwin's luxurious form of travel between the train and the hotel. Labeled "rapid transit in Beach Haven," a small trolley on train wheels runs through the marshes up to the oceanfront Baldwin with guests and their luggage. This train was pulled by a horse, which was not too much of a burden on the tracks.

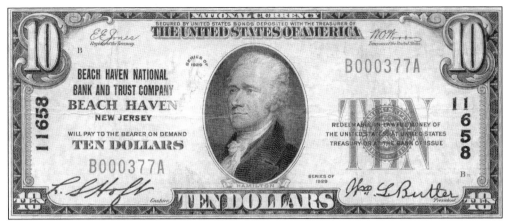

This specific bill was issued in 1929 by the Beach Haven National Bank and Trust Company. Referred to as "national currency," this money was used by nationally chartered local banks as their own currency. The reasoning behind this was that money that had the backing of the federal government just had to be good. Few of these bills are known to exist today and are rare collectibles.

If only taxes in Beach Haven could be the same as they were in 1904! J.B. Cox owned a general store that sold "staple and fancy groceries." He was assessed $22 in municipal taxes for his Beach Haven real estate, another $22 for the county tax, and $3.74 for the school tax, for a total of $47.74.

TAX NOTICE FOR 1904.

M _Ex J B. Cox_

To **BOROUGH OF BEACH HAVEN,** Dr.

A. W. SEVER, Collector, Beach Haven, N. J.

The Valuation of your Taxable Property for the year 1904
is as follows ;

Value of Real Estate,	$2200
Value of Personal Property,	$........
Total value,	$2200
Deduct for Debts,	$........
Total to be Assessed,	$2200

Your Assessment is divided as follows : —

Amount County Tax, @ $1.00 per $100.	$2200
" Borough Tax, @ 1.00 " "	$2200
" Spec. School Tax, @ 17c "	$374
" Poll Tax,	$........
" Dog Tax,	$........
" Postage,	$........
The total amount of your Tax for the year 1904 is	$4774

The above Tax is required to be paid on or before the 20th day of December, 1904, or to be returned according to law. Taxes not paid when due draw interest at the rate of 12 per cent. per annum until paid, to be collected with Tax.

The Commissioners of Appeal in case of taxation will meet in the Hopper Building, Beach Haven, on Tuesday, Oct. 25, 1904, for the purpose of discharging duties of their office; to whom all complaints concerning taxes should be made.

Please make checks payable to A. W. Sever, Collector.

Received the above Tax in full,

Collector.

Visit BEACH HAVEN!
The NEW OCEAN RESORT-7 Miles at Sea.
No Stifling Land Breezes!! Always Cool!!

Mrs. N. Gilson

Windsor

Box 35   *Vermont*

PRESERVE THE INCLOSED SCHEDULE OF TRAINS.

Promotion was in vogue—so were exaggeration and, maybe, outright lies. This envelope advertises that Beach Haven is now seven miles at sea in addition to "No stifling land breezes!! Always cool!" It is a rare artifact with the enclosed summer train schedule. The envelope is stamped October 1 from Tuckerton. The postage was 3¢ for the envelope and included the train schedule.

Everyone loves a parade, and the biggest on Long Beach Island was celebrated on June 20, 1914, when cars first drove over the new causeway. Everyone along the route waved and cheered as the cars slowly passed by. American flags and red, white, and blue bunting of all types adorned houses and cars along the side of the road, especially those participating in the parade.

In addition to flags on cars, creativity was the name of the game during parades. This driver can hardly see. With the car's steering wheel on the right side, he leans out to see through the decor, which includes both Beach Haven and Philadelphia pennants. Flowers cover the car. Frederick Ostendorf won for the best decorated car, and Joseph Shonders was honored for the best decorated home.

In this view looking south from the bay side of Beach Haven, one can see that Bay Avenue was a wilderness of blowing and unmanageable sand. With Beach Avenue being the focal point for the town, Bay Avenue was not built up until the mid-1920s. It was imperative that the railroad tracks be kept clear. Any problem with the tracks could stop train service for a day or two.

Center Avenue (now known as Centre Street) had some of the most exclusive cottages in town, second only to Coral Street. Stylish Victorians were large, with five to seven bedrooms for families and their servants. In the days before air-conditioning, front porches were in constant use for both relaxing and entertaining. Several of these homes were built for personal use by investors of the Baldwin Locomotive Works in Philadelphia. A number of these old Victorians still stand today in the historic preservation district.

Houses by this time were beginning to be outlined by fences. Most were on 50-by-100-foot lots or smaller as laid out by the Beach Haven Improvement Company back in the late 1800s. Of interest are the telephone poles that extend across the marshes and the roads that are still made of sand. Beach Haven's water tower in the far distance was photographed from the Baldwin Hotel.

The street in this postcard leads to the boardwalk overlooking the beach. Sadly, and unknowingly, most original sand dunes were taken down and used for roads and fill for lots. The investors of the Beach Haven Land and Improvement Company wanted most homes near the ocean to have water views. This idea would prove disastrous in later years when storms washed from ocean to bay.

Birds-Eye View   Beach Haven, N. J.

The Hotel Baldwin is at the far right, with its minarets standing out. In this photograph, Beach Avenue runs almost diagonally from top right to center left. Near Sea, the white house to the left of the Hotel Baldwin, on the southeast corner of Beach Avenue and Coral Street, belonged to Frederick Ostendorf, a restaurant owner from Philadelphia. He also built the huge Ostendorf Garage for car and boat storage.

Aerial views of Beach Haven were common, like this one showing the turreted Engleside on the right side of the postcard and the Hotel Baldwin to the left. A place to see and be seen, the boardwalk is clearly visible. Changing configuration and length a few times, it became the most popular place in town. Beach Haven has always been known as a family resort, placid and relaxing.

Postcards were a perfect way to advertise. Visitors wrote notes, sending them to friends and family. Taken from the air with a view looking west, this image shows the magnificent Engleside, established by Robert Barclay Engle in 1876 and taken over by his son Robert Fry Engle in 1901, when his father became ill. It catered to an exclusive group of guests.

Two

THE LURE OF THE SEA

CHILDREN THRIVE ON THE SUNNY STRAND

"Children thrive on the sunny strand," is the perfect ad for Beach Haven in the early 1900s and today too. Here, nine youngsters pose for a photographer. Sand, sun, salt water, and fun for all ages is without a doubt the best part of a summer vacation on this special barrier island. Suits are still wool but offer more freedom to the wearer and are short enough for him or her to play in the sand and ride waves.

The Beach Haven boardwalk was anywhere from a few inches to a few feet off the sand and had no safety railings, so it was easy to step from one spot to another. There were also walkways from the boardwalk to the beach. A few stores were on the boardwalk, but just walking close to the crashing waves on the pure white sand was enough for most people.

Children's Playground
Beach Haven, N. J.

In this late-1920s photograph, one youngster waits for a hole to be dug wide and deep enough so he can sail his toy boat. *Children's Playground* is a perfect title for this happy postcard. Beach Haven was the first taste of freedom for many young children. There were no rules—except to be considerate of others.

This is an early
photograph of two
girls hiking up
their skirts so they
would not get wet
and was found in
one of Robert Fry
Engle's personal
albums. People in
town knew Engle as
the proper Quaker
hotel proprietor
and photographer.
Along with his wife,
Sarah Atkinson,
he did not believe
in liquor and never
allowed it or a bar
in the Engleside.

A little girl is in deep thought as to what she is building in the sand almost directly under the
boardwalk. Dressed in her Sunday best, she is loading her tin buckets with white sugar sand high
up on the beach. A small wooden shovel helps her fill the painted buckets. It is obvious that she
does not care about getting her skirt, jacket, or shoes full of sand.

What did this little girl have in mind while she played by herself in the sand? Clothed in a dress, long stockings, and high boots, she was intent on making something known only to herself. Using a long metal shovel with wooden handle and a dark tin pail, she has already built two castles but does not seem satisfied.

Sand Dunes Beach Haven, N. J.

Sand Dunes, Beach Haven, N.J. is an unusual scene. The original town fathers wanted everyone in the first few houses from the ocean to have a water view, so existing sand dunes were leveled to provide sand for fill and streets. No one ever thought about the possibility of erosion or devastating storms, yet that was exactly what was happening on the next barrier island south called Tucker's Island.

Beach Scene. Beach Haven, N. J.

This postcard is simply titled *Beach Scene, Beach Haven, N.J.* The beach and ocean are packed with happy visitors. It is low tide and the waves are breaking extremely far out. A few wooden and canvas beach chairs are being used. How happy people must have been going from a hot, dry train ride to a perfect day on the beach and in the water.

THE IDEAL SLOPING BEACH — HERE EVEN THE CHILDREN ARE SAFE

"The ideal sloping beach—Here even the children are safe," states an advertisement for the beach in front of the Engleside. It sounds outdated now but was a clever ploy to get families to come to Beach Haven. Friends and families gather together at the water's edge in the 1920s to cool off on a hot summer day. Tank-type shirts are still part of the bathing costume.

There is depth is this photograph: dunes in the front to the left balanced with frothy white waves in the background. At the waterline, an adult and a small child can be seen. Are they collecting shells at the water's edge, or had Robert Fry Engle simply chosen a touching scene to photograph?

Unsuspecting children made up some of Robert Fry Engle's best photographs. Here, a young boy, probably looking for a flat area where he could play without waves or getting too wet, is pulling his toy sailboat with canvas sails in a wooden child's cart to the bay. This photograph is a bit fuzzy, but shows the corner of the original Beach Haven Yacht Club in the right-hand corner.

1 6 3

Robert Fry Engle's photograph shows two boys engrossed in a building project made from wood washed ashore. The ocean was full of pieces of wood that washed in from wrecks and off of overloaded decks. Such amusement nourished the overloaded imaginations of eager builders, engineers, and architects of the future. By the water's edge, an older girl throws a stick for two dogs.

A chauffeur or hotel employee leads a well-dressed couple with two little girls down the boardwalk. One of the exquisite Victorian lights, which were lit each evening and extinguished every morning by lamplighter Thomas Crane on his bicycle, is shown from its best angle. Fastened to the side of the boardwalk, each light did its job casting a glow almost to the center of the walkway.

Parasols were often used by ladies who did not want to get their skin harmed by the sun yet be stylish. The lady seen from the back is dressed in bold stripes, while a proper gentleman holds her arm. Walkways led from the Engleside and Baldwin to the boardwalk, and in turn, there were steps or walkways down to the sand where needed, depending on the height of the sand.

BEACH HAVEN, N.

Robert Fry Engle was proud of his panoramic photographs that were "panographed," according to the phrase used from the 1870s on. Engle's images were in an exhibit in Washington, DC, in 1896 and were praised by Alfred Stieglitz as the first American exhibit "worthy of international attention." Engle's photographs are also at the Smithsonian.

In 1901, the appearance between the Engleside and the beach could have been a bit more polished. As it was, there were only narrow wooden paths, a pavilion, and bathhouses that were provided for its guests. There were no lights on the boardwalk yet. Landscape and native plants were well in the future.

This photograph taken on a windy day shows Engleside Hotel umbrellas on their sides and people huddled under them. There is nothing but sand and American dune grass in the spaces between the Victorian "cottages," hotels, and the boardwalk, except for bathhouses, a tennis court, and narrow walkways. Oddly enough, children never played in the sand on the west side of the boardwalk.

Robert Fry Engle seemed to have had an affinity for photographs of people enjoying the beach and ocean for years. There are many taken from the boardwalk overlooking his domain. Had he ever thought of widening the narrow wooden walkway from boardwalk to beach? The tide is very high with a small tidal pool for youngsters to play in that is almost directly in front of the lifeguard stand.

From the shade in this photograph, it was taken around mid-morning. The walkway was covered with sand from the bathers. Of note in this picture are two wicker carriages that would now be considered museum quality. The smaller one probably has a baby sleeping in it covered with a light blanket, while the larger one holds a toddler who is playing in the sand.

By the mid-1930s, cover-ups were beginning to be shed. Men could sit on the sand or swim without shirts while ladies could walk the boardwalk in one-piece suits. This lady is walking her dog on a leash in the late 1930s. She is joined by a friend, also in a bathing suit. Both wear shoes to keep splinters out of their feet.

BOARDWALK AND BEACH LOOKING SOUTH, BEACH HAVEN, LONG BEACH, N. J.

This postcard is titled *Boardwalk and Beach Looking South, Beach Haven, Long Beach, N.J.* Simplistic as this sounds today, each postcard that was sent advertised the happiness and fun had by each visitor. Word spread quickly that Beach Haven was not only safe but also offered something for everyone.

Fur coats were in fashion, and these two ladies are proud of their looks, as they stroll the boardwalk just south of the fishing pier. In the background is the stately, large turret of the Engleside. Could this photograph have been taken on an Easter weekend when the spring wind was known to blow and the temperature was colder than on the mainland due to the lower ocean temperature? Fashion was of the utmost importance on the Beach Haven boardwalk.

Emily Lloyd Wilson founded the Beach Haven Beach Patrol and provided a fully equipped first-aid station in a small building located on the boardwalk between the Engleside and Hotel Baldwin. In 1916, Wilson was appointed to the board of health; in merely a year, she established the first Red Cross chapter on the island, which grew to a membership of 337.

Three lifeguards sit on the stand around 1920. The official Beach Haven Beach Patrol had gone from just two lifeguards in front of each hotel to being responsible for swimmers and all beachgoers from Holyoke Avenue in the south to the northern boundary of Seventh Street. They had a pushcart that looked like a stretcher filled with necessary medical equipment that could be moved up and down the boardwalk.

BEACH PATROL

A highly efficient corps of beach guards are on duty throughout the season.

Lifeguards practiced their rescue drills most every day all summer. The rescue boats made by VanSant and Co. in Atlantic City contained life buoys and long lengths of line so the guards could assist anyone that was pulled out to sea by rip currents. When Emily Wilson obtained her official town job, the beach patrol was enlarged and popular beach areas began to be guarded.

Two lifeguards watch the crowd from the Engleside stand in the early days. Lifeguards were provided by only the Engleside and Hotel Baldwin. A long rescue line is on a spool attached to a rescue board that can be paddled out by a lifeguard to save someone in distress.

A game of tug-of-war was taken seriously, with a large number of spectators watching from the beach and the boardwalk. The lifeguards' line from their rescue boat was used as the tug-of-war line. Back and forth the line moved, until a marked center spot had clearly been pulled far enough in one direction to declare the winner.

Two boys, and possibly their younger sisters or friends, use a lifeguard's rescue line. Children around the turn of the last century did not always wear suits but were in their play clothes complete with shoes, sneakers, and socks. Middies are worn by three of the children while one sports a tie.

Some sort of fort or castle is being constructed at the water's edge by a group of children, all of whom are in on the fun. Free for the taking and making was anything found on the beach. In spite of the Engleside and Hotel Baldwin regularly cleaning their respective beaches, there were bits of wood everywhere. Imaginations ran wild depending on what materials were available and what each child hoped to build.

On the beach are the essentials of rescue equipment. A small rescue skiff is flanked by two lifeguards. The oars are in the boat, and it is ready to be pushed into the water and rowed out to a swimmer in distress. Next to it is a rescue board, attached to a long line of rope on a spool, that is used to rescue one person at a time.

Robert Fry Engle's panoramic photograph, taken in the 1800s, depicts the Engleside as the most majestic building in town. With the hotel's size and proximity to the ocean, every room must have had an ocean or bay view and a window that opened to let in the cool breezes that came up every day around noon. In front of the hotel is a walkway to the boardwalk and beach.

Three

ROBERT BARCLAY ENGLE, ROBERT FRY ENGLE, AND THE ENGLESIDE HOTEL

How could anyone have known that a child who was born on March 6, 1834, in Hainesport, Burlington County, New Jersey, would grow up to build and own what would be, for a time, the largest hotel in Beach Haven? Robert Barclay Engle went to a local elementary school, then attended the Westtown Friends Boarding School in Westtown, Pennsylvania. In 1875, he moved to Beach Haven. Along with his cousin Samuel Engle, who provided much of the financial backing, he built the majestic Engleside.

The land for the Engleside, seen in this image taken from the southeast side of the hotel, was purchased on January 1, 1876, and construction quickly followed. Robert Barclay Engle was a West Jersey Quaker, full of energy and enthusiasm. It was said that he would do anything to keep his guests happy. There were originally two tennis courts, croquet, sailing, picnics, games, and cards on the beach.

Robert Barclay Engle was praised for his Quaker business sense and outgoing personality. He married Jane Darnell in 1857. They had two sons: David Darnell Engle (the elder) and Robert Fry Engle. Jane is referred to as his "estimable wife" in the *Biographical Review of Camden and Burlington Counties* written in 1897. She is credited for the Engleside "becoming the fashionable watering-place of the swell set of Philadelphia."

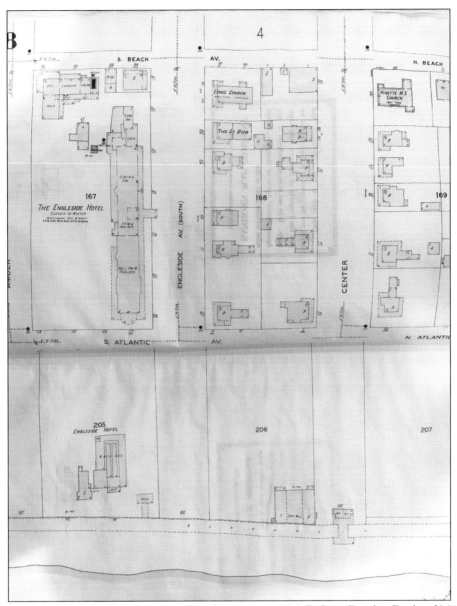

The Engleside was the first luxurious hotel to rise in 1876. Robert Barclay Engle of Mount Holly—once a teacher, then a farmer—found his true calling as proprietor of the Engleside Hotel in Beach Haven. The smaller Parry House was where Barclay had gotten a taste of running a hotel on a barrier island. Consequently, he was more than qualified to conquer the ins and outs of getting supplies and workers to build the Engleside Hotel. Sadly, the Parry House burned down in 1881, leaving the newly built Engleside to cater to the wealthy of Philadelphia. Shown on this Sanborn map, the Engleside took up a whole square block between Amber Street and Engleside Avenue and Atlantic and Beach Avenues. Nothing was built in front of the majestic hotel but the Engleside bathhouses, so there was a view from most every room. Behind the hotel were the laundry and rooms for the help. Homes and other establishments quickly sprang up around this focal point, with the Holy Innocents Episcopal Church (funded by a Mrs. Parry and named after her daughter who had died at age 19) built across the street.

Robert Barclay Engle and his son Robert Fry Engle always flew at least two American flags. A small one was between the beach walkway from the boardwalk and the lifeguard stand and was always leaning due to the wind, shifting sand, and children swinging on the pole. The large one was moved most every year as the hotel evolved. Both flagpoles stood upon tripods.

Tennis was very popular at the Engleside. Robert Fry Engle does not identify his subjects in this photograph, but they must have been good players to warrant a referee and an umpire who watched to ensure that they abided by the International Lawn Tennis Federation Rules of Tennis. At the Engleside, the chair umpire kept score and the referee stood next to him making official decisions.

William "Bill" Tilden, in the white coat, and his followers swooshed into the Engleside Hotel when it was at its finest. He gave as much as he got: fine performances in exchange for discounted rooms. His career spiraled upward, and he won six US National Championships in a row, along with a seventh a few years later. He absolutely dominated tennis in the 1920s and turned professional in 1930.

Robert Fry Engle took this photograph from the second or third shaded deck in the Engleside Tower. The tournament featured Bill Tilden on the south court and chairs with spectators lined up on both sides watching intently. Pity the young man on the northern court who had no one paying any attention to him.

A baseball game in the middle of the wide, sandy street—why not? Spectators line the front porch, rocking in wicker chairs, watching the fun coming from the street. Some of the teams even sat on the long bench in front of the Engleside steps. Most guest room windows were wide open on this extremely hot day. Sweet peas bloomed along the front lawn while fresh flowers were in all the public rooms.

Sundays were sometimes "Ladies' Softball Day," where men and women played together. To even things out, the men had to wear long skirts as a handicap. People from the proper Engleside roared. Daily fun was the name of the game for the Engleside, with the Engles leading the activities. One has to wonder who had more fun—the players or the spectators?

While there was no liquor allowed in the hotel, there was no lack of activities. When the causeway opened in June 1914, the Engleside was the nexus for the spectacular parade across the causeway and south for a celebration lunch. Robert Barclay Engle managed to get as many friends as possible to participate, including this car with a Beach Haven pennant hanging from the back.

From close-up, the Engleside was more classic and a better-looking hotel when compared to its rival the Baldwin across the sand. Plumbing and electricity did not come to Beach Haven until 1926. The water tower was erected in 1903. Residents and businesses used acetylene power and most had their own artesian wells with cisterns.

Everyone was properly dressed on festive occasions like the Fourth of July. In fact, the times decreed that there were no casual clothes. Wool pants and jackets with ties were normal hotel attire. The Engleside opened for guests on June 6, 1876. It had been a scramble bringing in lumber, with windows and doors mostly coming by boat from Camden. The Engleside Tower reached five stories high.

Cars seemed to follow no pattern or direction when parked outside the Engleside, with some even parked in the middle of the street. But who would have said anything to Robert Barclay Engle? He was well connected politically, had been a member of the Beach Haven Borough Council since its inception, and was elected senator on the Republican ticket.

Early Beach Haven security officers in front of the Engleside wore custodian helmets, headgear originally worn by English constables on foot patrol. Currently used by the Metropolitan Police Service in London, they are known as the "bobby on the beat" hats. Usually, there was a badge on the custodian hat with specific numbers identifying the officer.

There was competition between the Engleside and Baldwin Hotels as to which could provide the most unusual way to get from the station up to the oceanfront. The Hotel Baldwin tried a narrow-gauge trolley led by two horses. The Engleside settled on the Autocar bus made by the 1897 Pittsburgh Motor Vehicle Company. It could hold four people and cost $1,700.

This photograph is the only one known to exist that depicts the apparatus shown and has been debated by historians. This is thought to be a device that pumped salt water from the ocean up into the bathhouses so wool suits could have the sand removed and be washed off before being hung out on the lines to dry. Today, the practice sounds archaic, but at that time, bathing costumes were often rented rather than owned.

This photograph is one of Robert Fry Engle's best panoramic shots showing the open spaces and exclusivity of Beach Haven. What other seashore town on a cool, barrier island could have two magnificent hotels flanking large "cottages" built by the wealthy of Philadelphia? To the right is the Engleside. The popular Baldwin Hotel with minarets that could be seen for blocks graces the left side of this image.

Four

HOTEL BALDWIN AND OTHER ACCOMMODATIONS

Built in 1883, with Wilson Brothers as architects, the Baldwin Hotel was adorned with minarets and sided with cedar shakes. It was originally called the Arlington Inn. In 1885, Wilson's Baldwin Hotel in Bryn Mawr, Pennsylvania, burned down, and the rebuild was assigned to Frank Furness. The Baldwin in Bryn Mawr eventually became a private girls' school. With the name *Baldwin* left unused, the Wilson Brothers called this the New Hotel Baldwin.

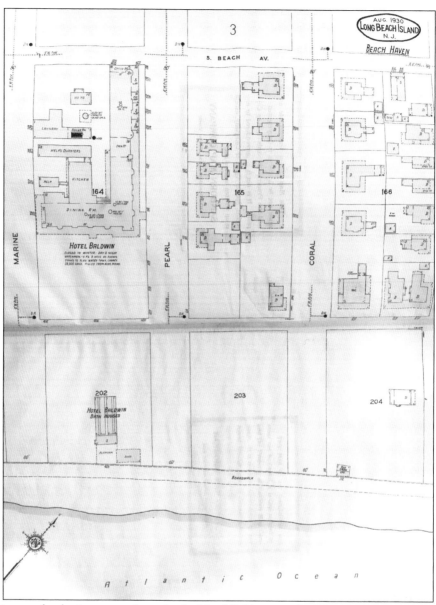

Catering to a fun-loving group of people, the Hotel Baldwin was built in 1883. The Quaker Engles did not believe in drinking, so there was never a bar at the Engleside. However, tea dances, croquet, tennis, and numerous activities provided fun for everyone. The Hotel Baldwin, as seen on this Sanborn map, also took up a square block just two blocks south of the Engleside. Described on this map as "closed in winter, watchman day and night," it was "connected to a 25,000 gallon water tank." During its many years of existence, the bar was the most popular place to relax after days of hunting, fishing, or relaxing on the beach, in addition to being a moneymaker. Early visitors came across the bay by steam yacht and were picked up by a little horse-drawn train running across the meadows and up to the hotel. In 1886, the Tuckerton Railroad came to Beach Haven; in 1914, the causeway was finished. Age took its toll on the Hotel Baldwin, but World War II troops gave the bar a new boost. A fire in 1947 was controlled by 10 fire companies; a 1960 fire, which could not be contained, resulted in the end of the glory days of the Hotel Baldwin.

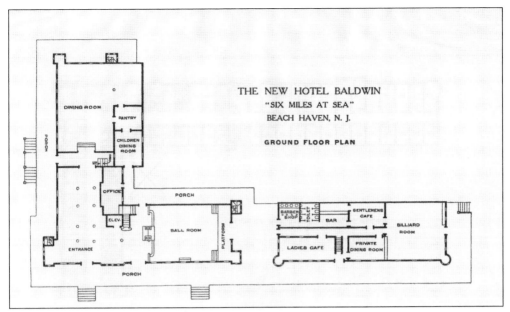

THE NEW HOTEL BALDWIN

"SIX MILES AT SEA"

BEACH HAVEN, N. J.

GROUND FLOOR PLAN

The New Hotel Baldwin "Ground Floor Plan" was laid out in an "L" shape. Facing the ocean on the northeastern side was the large lobby filled with comfortable wicker chairs in sitting areas separated by pillars. Next to the lobby were the dining room and children's dining room. Along Pearl Street were the large ballroom, a barbershop, ladies' café, a small private dining room, and a billiard room.

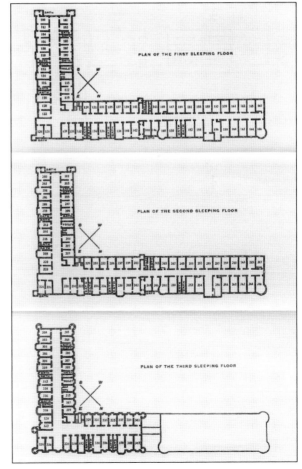

Plans of the three sleeping floors were stark, with bedrooms being anywhere from three to eight rooms away from the nearest bathroom. Guests at the Baldwin were more active; the hotel offered several activities not available at the Engleside. In addition to the billiard room, there were two bowling alleys and either gunning or trapshooting at the Corinthian Gun and Yacht Club on Saturday mornings in the open space south of the hotel.

Most of the porches have disappeared in this image of the Hotel Baldwin, looking in need of a lot of maintenance in the 1920s. Like the Engleside, it had a bathhouse for its guests to use to change into bathing suits and back into their clothes. Owner Mercer Baird was afraid of sand clogging up the pipes. Like the Engleside, the Hotel Baldwin had both fresh and salt water that ran through its pipes.

By 1912 salt, storms, and sand had taken their toll on the magnificent hotel. Real and ornamental Atlantic white cedar decks were rotten, and removed for safety. The hotel was showing its age; the revenue was coming in slowly. Sadly, the days of the big hotels were going downhill fast.

While the Engleside Hotel attracted the Philadelphia and New Jersey Quaker elite, the Baldwin drew those who wanted fun. This selection of cards portrays the elegance of the Hotel Baldwin, advertising it as the "Leading Summer Resort and Hotel," with "Hot and cold sea water bathing." Just a few years after this display of cards was published, the rest of the minarets fell in storms or rotted away.

An eloquent embossed invitation was sent to members of the Long Beach Board of Trade requesting their presence for dinner on Friday, July 11, 1919, at 7:00 p.m. at the Hotel Baldwin "in celebration of the extension of the Long Beach Boulevard to Barnegat City, NJ." Acceptances were to be mailed to the chairman, Honorable Leon Maja Berry, Court House Square Building, Camden, New Jersey.

The Long Beach Board of Trade

requests the honour of your presence

at a Dinner

to be given on Friday evening, the eleventh of July, nineteen hundred and nineteen

at seven o'clock

The Hotel Baldwin
Beach Haven, New Jersey

in celebration of the extension of the Long Beach Boulevard to Barnegat City, N. J.

Please send acceptance with check before July 5th, to
Hon. M. L. Berry, Chairman
Court House Square Building
Camden, New Jersey

Dinner Ticket, $2.50 each

At a time when it seemed as if everyone smoked, matchboxes were important PR handouts for hotels and restaurants. "Right on the Beach, Six Miles at Sea" got attention from those desiring a cool, summer vacation with fishing, sailing, gunning, and a lot of partying. An illustration of the Baldwin Hotel, Beach Haven, New Jersey, was on the front of each matchbox along with the direction "close cover before striking."

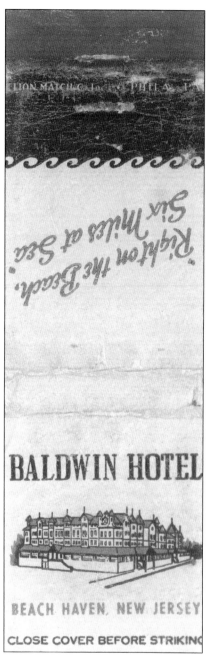

The inside of the matchbox provided the Hotel Baldwin's special contacts: "For reservations 3-7101, to call guests Beach Haven 3-9891 or Beach Haven 3-9851." Mercer Baird died during the 1920s, thus missing all that he lived for: the parties, self-indulgence, and prestige that he sought. The 1920s continued with Little Egg Harbor Yacht Club parties and assorted theme dances held at the Hotel Baldwin.

By the late 1930s, it was obvious that the Hotel Baldwin was going the way of the Engleside. Jessie and Erving Townsend owned the hotel in the 1930s. They took out the popular tennis courts and replaced them with a miniature golf course. The hotel was stark white with none of its ornamentation left.

The first fire to strike the Hotel Baldwin occurred on the afternoon of August 9, 1947. Fortuitously, there was a convention of fire chiefs staying at the hotel that weekend who competently led the brigade. Having begun in a second-floor bedroom over the dining room, the fire was fully extinguished in two hours. Forty-four rooms were closed, and part of the dining room was destroyed.

The old hotel barely survived its first fire in 1947. Rooms were closed off, and food was served in the ballroom. The damage from this fire was estimated at about $75,000. One of the fire trucks was advertising a carnival to be held that night. The Hotel Baldwin was just about at its end, with less revenue coming in each summer.

Hoses remain draped from the roofs and rooms of the Hotel Baldwin. Exhausted and heroic volunteers from both the Fire Chief's Convention and the local Beach Haven Volunteer Fire Company lean against the fire trucks. Amazingly, they managed to contain a fire that could have destroyed several blocks of Beach Haven.

The last fatal fire at the Hotel Baldwin occurred the night of September 24, 1960. This time there was a heavy east wind, which could have taken not only the Hotel Baldwin but also a number of houses within four blocks. This fire was fought by companies from Toms River south to Pleasantville all to no avail. The old wooden hotel from 1883 burned to the ground. Flames could be seen for miles. People flocked to inspect the smoldering embers the next day as firemen remained on duty. Hoses are seen spraying down the last of the fire. Homes in the block from Beach Avenue to Bay Avenue were spared thanks to courageous firemen. Spectators drove for miles to view not only the last of a spectacular fire but also the last of what was once a beautiful oceanfront structure decorated with minarets, the Hotel Baldwin. The property was sold to the Holy Innocents Episcopal Church the next year, after it had been cleared.

Acme Hotel, Beach Haven, N. J.

John Cranmer moved the Philip Dunn cottage out to the end of Dock Road in Beach Haven near the Hotel de Crab. After building a lot on the west side, he found huge success in the Acme. Rooms and additions were added. The result was the 1904 Acme Hotel. The Acme became instantly popular and has continued to remain so under different ownership and name.

Hotel Acme, Beach Haven, N. J.

This postcard advertises "Hotel Acme," but this horse trolley was owned and run by the Hotel Baldwin. It made the run from the bay steamboat stop and the Acme Hotel to the oceanfront Hotel Baldwin. The horsecar took Baldwin guests on the narrow-gauge line to the Beach Haven Yacht Club, Acme Hotel, and other stops along the way.

This sign reads Acme Hotel Grill Bar Restaurant. In 1925, the Acme was owned by the colorful and popular Gustave "Ernie" Tueckmantel, who left a legend of success. Stories of outwitting the Coast Guardsmen during Prohibition and always-plentiful liquor were passed from generation to generation.

To the left, the sign announces the headquarters of the Beach Haven Marlin and Tuna Club, while a sign advertising the Acme Hotel's bar/grill offering "Clam Chowder – Sandwiches – all kinds" decorates the right. Ernie Tueckmantel and his wife, Hannah, began to get competition from his brothers, Gus and Whitey, who started the popular Gus and Whitey's Restaurant, now Tucker's. At about 60, Ernie retired and sold to Bird and Betty Clutter, pictured here, who found they could make money in the bar business.

The Acme Hotel was one of the earliest buildings on the bay side. It became a rather fancy place to be seen, with Ernie Tueckmantel filling flower boxes, spreading out rocking chairs for relaxation, and selling Reid's Popular ice cream. After Prohibition, patrons still found the hotel, restaurant, and all of Dock Road a popular area.

Hotel DeCrab, Beach Haven, N. J.   Published by A. J. Durand.

Capt. Tilton Fox had this building— once a house of refuge and instrumental in the operation of the US Life-Saving Service in Harvey Cedars—brought by barge down to Beach Haven on Mud Hen Creek abutting Dock Road. On the top floor were iron beds for hunters and fishermen. Fox's friends teased him about his rather low-class accommodations, so he facetiously called his boardinghouse the Hotel de Crab.

The Hotel de Crab was a popular, less formal hangout from 1873, when it was towed down Barnegat Bay to Little Egg Harbor Bay and placed on top of cedar pilings along Mud Hen Creek. Before the construction and arrival of trains in 1886, barges and large catboats brought building materials, food, and sundry supplies to the landing at the end of the creek.

The Spray Beach House was built along the railroad line. It was a small 12-bedroom hotel built in the dunes overlooking the ocean, with almost no buildings around it. Philadelphian Augustus Keil purchased the Spray Beach House in 1908. He was instrumental in getting the causeway built in 1914 and became the first president of the board of trade. The Spray Beach House on Twenty-Third Street was sold to the Pitcairn Company in 1916.

The stately Beach Haven House stood at the northeast corner of Bay Avenue and Center Avenue, now called Centre Street. On land he purchased from the Tuckerton and Long Beach Land and Improvement Company, Lloyd Jones built the hotel in late 1874. The accommodations at the Beach Haven House were sparse, with the bare minimum of a bed, chair, washstand, and chamber pot.

1248   Beach Haven House, Beach Haven, N. J.

In 1890, Henry Mulholland purchased the Beach Haven House, raising it above the marsh to protect patrons from mosquitoes and flies. In the 1930s, Richard Lamb Jr., of Mount Holly, purchased the Beach Haven House and moved it to an adjoining lot, where it remained until being demolished in 1967. A new restaurant was built on the original site and sold to the Buckalew family in 1949. It remains in operation today as Buckalew's Restaurant and Bar.

865   The Biltmore and Bay Avenue, Beach Haven, N. J.

The resort town of Beach Haven was growing by leaps and bounds. It could accommodate people of all financial means and backgrounds. While the elite tended to build large "cottages" or stayed at the Engleside or Hotel Baldwin, smaller places were just as much fun and less costly. The Biltmore advertised a few rooms and meals. It still stands today, looking as it always has, on the west side of Bay Avenue between Second and Third Streets.

The St. Rita Hotel, located next to the Long Beach Island Historical Association Museum (formerly Holy Innocents Episcopal Church) on Engleside Avenue, was built by Frank Walker as his residence and Beach Haven's first post office. It was sold to the Dease family, then to Herb Feiler, and ultimately to its present owner, Marie Coates. During World War II, the hotel housed troops sent to protect Long Beach Island.

The Magnolia House was one of the first boardinghouses in Beach Haven. To construct this large rooming house, wood was barged over from the mainland by first owner Hiram Lamson. The boardinghouse was then sold to the Conklin family, who ran it for many years. Charter boat captains, their mates, and other seasonal workers lived in a big room on the third floor. This building has been remodeled several times and still stands on Centre Street.

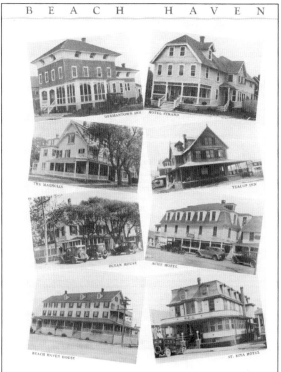

A potpourri of eight images of Beach Haven's hotels and boardinghouses portrays the popularity of the town during the early 1900s–1930s. The top left is mismarked; it was once the Hotel Strand and is now a private home. The Acme Hotel is a popular night spot for partygoers, and the St. Rita is still in business, though sparsely rented. The Beach Haven House was located where Buckalew's Restaurant is today.

Five

RESIDENTS AND THE BEACH HAVEN COMMUNITY

Charles Beck was a major player in the building of Beach Haven and the causeway for cars in 1914. He was active in politics and known for entertaining wealthy friends. He spent a lot of time at "the Farm" in Beach Haven, where he hunted, fished, farmed, and spent time dredging the southern end of Mordecai Island. This photograph is captioned, "The Residence of Charles W. Beck."

Our old cottage

By the mid-1920s, the Victorian Cottages were outnumbered by simpler, classic summer residences with cedar siding, shutters, and large porches. Few houses were constructed east of Atlantic Avenue (right side of photograph), so this could have been considered oceanfront. By the 1920s, cars were extremely popular on the island, even though most roads were sand or gravel.

RICHARD LAMB, PROP., BEACH HAVEN HOUSE, BEACH HAVEN, N. J.

While not as classy as the Engleside or Baldwin, the Beach Haven House was located on the corner of Bay Avenue and Centre Street. Conveniently located at the headwaters of Mud Hen Creek, it was first a small hotel and school. Proprietor Richard Lamb bought the 1874 Bayview House in 1883 and changed the name to Beach Haven House. It was torn down in 1949, and its former location is now the site of Buckalew's popular restaurant and bar.

By the 1920s, Beach Haven had been "found," and houses of all types and sizes were being constructed. The St. Louis House, on Bay and Norwood Avenues, was constructed of cinder blocks on the first floor; there were asbestos squares on the front second floor and cedar shake siding on the dormers. Stucco surrounded a third-floor diamond-shaped window.

The "Beautiful Residential District" described on this postcard was immaculate, with stately homes along Atlantic Avenue (left). These homes included single-car garages, hydrangeas, seaside foliage, awnings with open or screened porches for summer breezes, and sidewalks. In the background are the Baldwin Hotel and the water tower.

The St. Louis House, Bay and Norwood Aves.
Beach Haven, New Jersey

31075

Beautiful Residential District
Beach Haven, N. J.

The House Boat Colony, Beach Haven, N. J.

The Beach Haven houseboat colony was usually towed over from the mainland every summer and served as the homes for workers such as captains, hotel employees, and mates on boats. Families lived in close quarters with kerosene lamps and a complete lack of sanitation. In 1926, Beach Haven was the first town in New Jersey to ban houseboats because of their sanitation problems.

BUSINESS SECTION, LOOKING SOUTH, BEACH HAVEN, LONG BEACH, N.J.

By the 1930s, Bay Avenue had been paved and many stores had been added. Both diagonal and horizontal parking were allowed. The tall white building on the right is Harry Colmer's Colonial Movie Theatre. An electrician from Camden, Colmer built the theater in 1922 to play the silent movies of the time. Cranmer's Lumber Company built the four sides, which were then moved to the site and tethered together.

Marshall's Restaurant, Beach Haven, N. J.

Captain John Marshall and his wife opened a small restaurant to the east of the Beach Haven Yacht Club named Marshall's. "Prices reasonable, satisfaction guaranteed" proclaimed a sign above the front porch. Marshall also advertised garage and boat storage. Rocking chairs provided relaxation for patrons waiting to rent boats.

Parker's Houseboats and Restaurant on Dock, Beach Haven, N. J.

Purchased by Ellis and Liz Parker, Marshall's was renamed Parker's Grill in the early 1900s. It was later demolished by Ellis and his son, Tuck, who built Parker's Boat Garage at Dock Road and West Avenue. The MacArthur family ran the boat garage next, and it was then converted by Bill and DeeDee Lutz into a restaurant named the Boat House, later run by Tony and Patty Baldino. Today, it is a popular restaurant known as Parker's Garage and Oyster Saloon.

Colonial Theatre
Where only the best moving pictures are shown.

The era of movies in Beach Haven began with silent films played at the former school building on Third Street. It had a hand-generated projector accompanied by Freida Joorman Cranmer giving a loud rendition of music from the piano. Movies were shown four nights a week. As movie popularity increased, Harry Colmer and Leon Cranmer bought property on the corner of Bay Avenue and Centre Street. They built a large building; the walls were prefabricated across the street at Cranmer Lumber Company. It opened on July 4, 1922. In the hot days of summer, ice was placed in front of the theater for a cool breeze. Colmer, originally from Camden, soon became the sole proprietor, working along with his wife and family over the years. Generations of moviegoers remember a dark red velvet curtain that opened, a balcony full of noisy teenagers, and the latest movies available, thanks to the nonstop energy and innovations of Harry Colmer. This building still stands and is used today as a retail store.

After the 1944 hurricane, seaweed and trash cluttered the streets. But the theater survived, as did Harry Colmer's second endeavor, the Colonial Theatre in Brant Beach, which was built in the late 1920s. He had a third theater in Barnegat, which was once an old opera house where he showed movies. People marveled at Colmer's energy and ability to change the movies most every night. He drove from location to location to deliver cans of film. During World War II, each night the movie opened with a picture of the American flag, followed by the singing of the national anthem. Colmer's prices were always kept on the low side, designed to attract as many moviegoers as possible. Before the main feature, there were newsreels, a cartoon, and previews of movies to come. During the war, troops went to the movies whenever possible. If sirens rang, the troops marched out to their drills. Colmer died in 1956, but his family ran the theaters for another eight years before selling them.

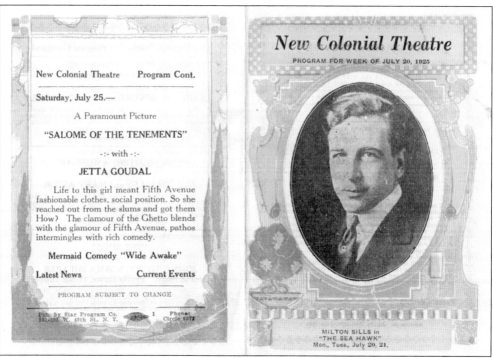

New Colonial Theatre Program Cont.

Saturday, July 25.—

A Paramount Picture

"SALOME OF THE TENEMENTS"

-:- with -:-

JETTA GOUDAL

Life to this girl meant Fifth Avenue fashionable clothes, social position. So she reached out from the slums and got them How? The glamour of the Ghetto blends with the glamour of Fifth Avenue, pathos intermingles with rich comedy.

Mermaid Comedy "Wide Awake"

Latest News   Current Events

PROGRAM SUBJECT TO CHANGE

Pub. by Star Program Co.   Phone:
201-203 W. 49th St., N. Y.   Circle 6073

New Colonial Theatre

PROGRAM FOR WEEK OF JULY 20, 1925

MILTON SILLS in
"THE SEA HAWK"
Mon., Tues., July 20, 21.

Harry Colmer never missed handing out his brochures with shows for the week. This brochure advertises Hamilton Sills in *The Sea Hawk* to be shown Monday and Tuesday, July 20 and 21, 1925. Colmer's shows were extremely popular. He stood almost six and a half feet tall with an enormous appetite for local Britz's ice cream and known for devouring a whole pie at each sitting.

NEW COLONIAL THEATRE
Beach Haven, N. J.

Show Starts at 7:15 and 9:15 Daylight Time
At 6:15 and 8:15 Standard Time

Admission: Adults 50c; Children under 10 years 20c

PROGRAM

Monday and Tuesday, July 20 and 21—

Attraction Extraordinary

Rafael Sabatini's immortal romance, featuring

"THE SEA HAWK"

Rafael Sabatini's immortal romance, featuring

MILTON SILLS

The most dramatic and fascinating story ever written by Rafael Sabatini, author of "Scaramouche," "Captain Blood" and others. Fourteen brilliant stars in the cast. The most extraordinary settings ever built of a motion picture. Over three thousand slaves, sailors and fighting men engaged in a naval battle on the high seas. Four largest ships ever built, at a cost of $285,000 for a motion picture in actual combat. An entire Algerian city, with its slave market erected for "The Sea Hawk." More than $85,000 worth of gorgeous gowns and costumes. Galley slaves shown for the first time. Barbary corsairs and the piracy of Spanish and English buccaneers. A million dollar production with every cent of expense evident on the screen.

Pathe Comedy   International News

Shows Start at 7:00 and 9:15 D. L. T.

Admission: Adults 50c—Children 35c

New Colonial Theatre   Program Continued

Wednesday, July 22—Warner Bros. present

"THE NARROW STREET"

With a special cast, including

DOROTHY DEVORE and MATT MOORE

Out of the blinding storm and into his bachelor quarters—in a quaint little narrow street—stumbled this beautiful girl of mystery. From then on things of which he had never dared to dream began to happen.

A 2 reel Comedy

Thursday, July 23—Carl Laemmle presents

"THE FIGHTING AMERICAN"

— featuring —

PAT O'MALLEY and MARY ASTOR

First in peace, first in action, first in the hearts of his lady-loves. That's Bill Pendleton, hero of "The Fighting American." Talk about romance, thrills, adventure! This picture is packed with all three.

Comedy "The Aggravating Kid"

Friday, July 24.—Metro-Goldwyn presents

"THE SNOB"

With a cast of artists, featuring

JOHN GILBERT, NORMA SHEARER
Conrad Nagel, Phyllis Haver, Hedda Hopper

Women adored him — the social world that he fawned upon thought him perfectly charming. The ladies were literally at his feet. His wife despised him. And his wife? Well, he never mentioned the fact he had one.

PROGRAM CONTINUED ON FOURTH PAGE

Admission to the Colonial Theatre was 50¢ for adults and 35¢ for children. Most nights there were shows at 7:00 p.m. and 9:00 p.m., each with a short comedy and newsreel. His brochures read like an opening sentence of suspense: "Out of the blinding storm and into his bachelor quarters—in a quaint little narrow street— stumbled this beautiful girl of mystery."

Post Office and Hall's Store at Beach Haven, N. J.

This postcard shows visitors outside Hall's Store and the post office at Centre Street and Beach Avenue (now Show Place Ice Cream Parlor). In the early 1900s, women were properly clad in long summer dresses with hats to protect them from the sun. Little boys were in shorts and knee socks and hats. This postcard promotes the new town of Beach Haven with a post office and nice stores—even though the roads were made of oil-coated gravel.

Floyd Cranmer was one of the most popular and successful builders on the island from 1925 to 1954. Almost obscured by a car, he is shown here fixing a window on the front of the new Beach Haven Post Office. This post office was built in 1950, with air-conditioning added in 1954. Harry Willits was postmaster.

U. S. POST OFFICE, Fifth St. & Bay Avenue.   Photo from Lynn Photo Service

Floyd Cranmer is visible at the right, working at the window. In 1950, Floyd L. Cranmer submitted the successful bid to construct a post office building and to lease it to the USPS. Harry Willits was the postmaster at that time. In 1954 air conditioning was added to the building for no increase in the rent. An addition was put on the rear of the building, in 1960 by Edward Nees, as Mr. Cranmer had passed away in 1954. In 1968, the front of the building was renovated adding a brick veneer panel, new signage and a curtain wall window treatment. The building was made barrier free in 1997, with the addition of a ramp and a new entrance on the north side of the building.

THE PHARO MEMORIAL LIBRARY

This historic building is one of the finest examples of its type of architecture on the whole Atlantic seaboard.

Built in 1924, the Beach Haven Library looks identical today. Owner of the first home in town on Second Street, Archelaus Pharo and his family donated the land behind their property for the library. Designed by renowned architect Brognard Okie, it has two fireplaces on the first floor and a high cathedral ceiling. The latest best sellers, a children's area, DVDs, and many other books are on the first floor. In the back room are computers and printers for residents and visitors to use. The second floor has a museum in the back room, which contains many documents related to the history of Beach Haven, numerous binders on the town's history, and artful displays in glass cases. There are hotel registers, deeds, diaries, and many items relating to Beach Haven's past. The library is now a building for the whole community: there are adult and children's programs, lectures, a reading group, reading hours for children, and a knitting group. With friendly and knowledgeable librarians, the Beach Haven Library is still the pride of Beach Haven.

Six

RELIGION AND EDUCATION IN BEACH HAVEN

The view in this postcard of the Holy Innocents Episcopal Church and St. Rita Hotel to the east (right) on Engleside looks much as it did a half century ago. Built in 1882, the church was damaged during a storm, and a winter chapel was added. In 1974, a new Holy Innocents Church was built on the site where the Hotel Baldwin had stood. The St. Rita was once a hotel owned by the Dease family. It was ultimately sold to Marie Coates, who still runs it today.

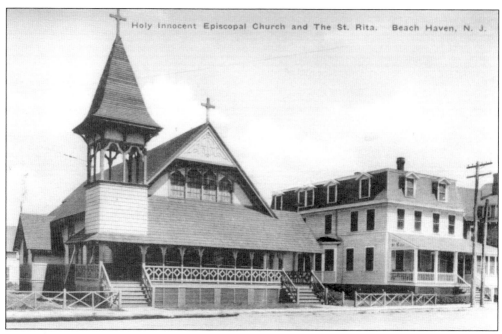

An early postcard of the Holy Innocents Episcopal Church shows a fence running from the front steps along a sandy Beach Avenue. Today, the building is the Long Beach Island Historical Association Museum and is filled with artifacts of the island. Events, including the popular Monday night summer lectures, are run by a team of dedicated volunteers who keep the facility in pristine shape.

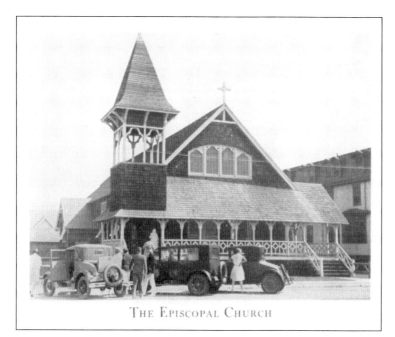

THE EPISCOPAL CHURCH

Parishioners attend Sunday services and weddings at the Holy Innocents Episcopal Church in Beach Haven. This photograph was taken in the late 1920s. Charles Parry and his wife donated money to build the church after the Parry House Hotel fire. Mrs. Parry named it "for all children in paradise," after children, like her stillborn baby, who died before their parents.

ROMAN CATHOLIC CHURCH

St. Thomas Roman Catholic Church on the corner of Fourth Street and Beach Avenue was originally a seasonal church without a full-time priest. It was so small, approximately 30 by 70 feet, that an overflow of parishioners would stand on the steps or outside the windows hoping to hear mass. The first full-time priest, who had lived at the Hotel Baldwin, was Fr. William Gilfillan. His successor, Fr. Thomas Joseph Whelan, oversaw the building of the rectory. The land for the Beach Haven Catholic church cost $450, and the architect was Edward Durang of Philadelphia. It was constructed by William Butler, Beach Haven's first mayor, who built many prominent structures in the town. The cost to build it was $4,000. Catherine Isabella Sprague, daughter of Jeremiah and Mary Sprague, was the first baby to be baptized at St. Thomas. In 1928, the church was taken over by the Franciscan priests, who were always seen in brown wool robes and sandals.

75

St. Thomas Aquinas Roman Catholic Church was built in 1899 on the corner of Fourth Street and Beach Avenue. Mass was originally held in the Third Street school or at summer homes. By 1890, priests from Lakewood conducted two masses on Sundays and holy days. The Rev. Thomas B. Healey was the first full-time priest. The building stands today, locked up and used as a storage unit.

Methodist Church, Beach Haven, N. J.

The Kynett Methodist Church was originally located on Beach Avenue, between Second and Centre Streets. The Quaker Meeting House, once Beach Haven's first library, was moved from Second Street and placed beside the Methodist church in 1904. In March 1932, fire destroyed the original Kynett Methodist Church. A new church was built and was dedicated in August 1933 on the corner of Centre Street and Beach Avenue.

This photograph of the Kynett Methodist Church was taken in September 1903 after a storm had knocked off the tall steeple. Interesting is the "X Our Place," which must denote the owners' house of worship. This first year-round church was moved a bit southward on Beach Avenue and still holds services today. The Quaker Meeting House was added to enlarge the Methodist church.

The first Methodist church was built on Beach Avenue in 1891 and named after Dr. Alpha Jefferson Kynett, head of the Methodist General Conference. Beach Haven's first year-round church steeple was knocked off in 1903 by a storm. A fire ravaged the church in 1932, and it was then rebuilt a bit southward in 1933.

First M. E. Church

BEACH HAVEN SCHOOL

Beach Haven's first half-dozen children were taught at the Beach Haven House Hotel on Bay Avenue. In 1885, the growing number of children were moved to a building on Third Street. By 1905, there were 301 year-round residents, resulting in the 1912 construction of the redbrick school seen here in 1928. The Beach Haven Elementary School celebrated its 100th anniversary in 2012. It encompasses a whole block between Beach and Bay Avenues on Eighth Street. Today, it houses prekindergarten through sixth grade. Middle- and upper-school children are bused to the mainland schools of Stafford School District.

Seven

SAILING LITTLE EGG HARBOR BAY

Little Egg Harbor Bay was normally peppered with sailboats—mainly gaff-rigged, one-masted, wide-beamed catboats. These versatile vessels easily went from workboats laden with building materials to chartered pleasure cruises for visitors and summer residents, and eventually to sailboat racing.

Robert Fry Engle took this photograph from the water aboard a catboat. Other sailboats are tied up at the dock to the left. A large sailboat is moored in the water. Directly ahead is the Beach Haven Yacht Club. To the right is the Acme Bar and Grill, with John Tilton Fox's Hotel de Crab on the far right. The town was sparsely built on the bay side.

Tied up at the Beach Haven Yacht Club dock, this large catboat has a makeshift canvas cabin, which was used to protect ladies and children from both the sun and salt spray on rough days. Many of these cabins were made of canvas that could be rolled up or down at will.

The dock at the Beach Haven Yacht Club was shaped like a new moon, allowing each boat to land into the wind. The large canvas sail was dropped, allowed to dry, and, finally, furled and tied to the boom. The boat was then moved down the dock to allow other captains to land safely and smoothly. Children were available to bail and wash down the boats for a small fee.

Slowing down the boat and bringing it almost to a stop is accomplished by dropping the gaff so it is parallel to the deck. Then the captain heads the boat up into the wind, and it moves bow first into the dock. Usually, a mate or someone on the dock is there to tie up. The catboat on the left side of this photograph is coming into the dock.

At the end of the day, catboats sails are dried, furled, and held with sail ties. Lines are coiled and the boat is shipshape, ready for the next working day. The boats are tied to the dock from the bow while an anchor is thrown from the stern to hold the boat off the dock. Here, well-dressed captains discuss their sailing plans as a youngster looks on.

From the look of the American flag and the set of the sail on the boat tied to the dock, the wind is from the northeast. This photograph shows the curved dock that was taken up each winter, to avoid being damaged by ice and heavy wind, only has a few boats tied up. This photograph was taken when other captains were out with groups sailing or fishing.

Three catboats are moored off the bay side of Beach Haven. The waters were not deep, allowing the shallow draft, centerboard catboats to skim across the bay. The catboat to the left is for racing and fun for two people; it is probably about 15 feet long. In the center and to the right are bigger catboats for transporting goods from the mainland to Beach Haven. Robert Fry Engle has carefully composed this image so the shadows of the masts are reflected in the water beneath them. The sails have been furled and tied to their booms. There is no wind, and the water is like glass. Clouds in the background suggest the wind may pick up during the day. All catboats had centerboards that went up and down so these boats could sail in shallow or deep water. Catboats were strictly bay boats, used in all New Jersey coastal communities.

This photograph was taken from the marshes where West Avenue and Amber Street are today. A few sailboats are anchored and not in use while others are racing behind Mordecai Island in Little Egg Harbor Bay, headed for a buoy south of Mordecai. The bay was constantly filled with sailboats used for commercial or personal use.

A lone bayman sculls his sneakbox to a dock with a long oar used for both propulsion and direction. He could have spent the day hunting by himself. Hunters in similar sneakboxes were led out to the marshy islands, where they would lie down in the boat and wait until the birds were near.

Avid hunter Robert Fry Engle took this photograph among the marshy islands between Great Bay and Little Egg Harbor. Telephone poles that went from Tuckerton to Little Beach are seen in the background. A rowing sneakbox, strictly for hunting, is pulled up on the mud while the catboat that towed the sneakbox is anchored in deeper water.

This photograph taken by Robert Fry Engle in the early 1900s shows how beautiful the Atlantic coast looked before it was built up. Two lifeboats are visible: one on the beach and another anchored just into the water. A catboat with cabin is also anchored behind it while another sails away. The location could be Tucker's Island to the south.

Marked No. 14 in an album of Robert Fry Engle photographs, this image shows six catboats filled with people out for an excursion. Engle has captured a row of billowy clouds behind them. There is little wind as the canvas sails are loose and hanging from the gaff. There are only small ripples on the water; it was no doubt a gorgeous day of sailing on Little Egg Harbor Bay.

Robert Fry Engle liked to experiment with his photographs. Note the reflection of the sun and the shadows from the catboats on the calm water. From one of his albums, this photograph is marked No. 128. The clouds in the background complete the timeless picture.

The sailboat at anchor with small skiff tied behind seems to be a committee boat preparing for a race. Catboats are running the line in preparation for the start. The sun is peeking through the clouds on a misty day. Skilled photographer Robert Fry Engle captured many photographic moments like this on Little Egg Harbor Bay.

Even though he was running a large hotel, Robert Fry Engle still made time to experiment with his photography and do most of the developing himself. This photograph shows a bright moon coming through the clouds. He found beauty all around him, from the ocean to the bay, taking many of the same scenes over and over.

A catboat full of visitors sails on a perfect summer day. The sail is held up by the gaff, which is attached to the top of the mast through a pulley. To flatten the sail, the gaff is pulled tight. For a fuller sail, it is dropped a bit. In an emergency, such as a storm, the gaff can be let down until it is parallel with the boom or even dropped completely along with the boom until both reach the deck. The boat could then be anchored to wait out the storm. The other lines seen attached to the mast are lazy jacks, into which the whole sail rig falls. These were designed to keep the extra-large catboat sail from landing all over the deck. Local boatbuilders constructed catboats of all sizes with great proficiency. Yet, when they began to be raced seriously in the late 1800s, owners looked to the Herreshoff Boat Works in Bristol, Rhode Island, where naval architect, designer, and builder Nathanael Herreshoff was known for his quality racing boats.

Good captains wanted their sailing parties on Little Egg Harbor Bay to feel comfortable. So, a reef was taken in the heavy canvas sail; the gaff was dropped partially and lines tied the excess sail to the boom, thus decreasing the amount of sail area. It made for an easier sail so customers would not get too wet or bounced around on a windy day.

The boat of choice since Beach Haven began was a versatile catboat. Some looked like large barges designed to carry building supplies and people. With a large, full sail, adjustable gaff and centerboard, this small catboat was used strictly for racing. Properly rigged, it could easily be handled by one person.

Robert F. Engle captures the spirit of catboat racing in this photograph. Taken from a distance, it shows catboats of all sizes on Little Egg Harbor Bay. When two or more sailboats get close together, it is natural for each to go as fast as possible and outsail the other boat. Both adjust the sail, raise or lower the centerboard, and try to get ahead of the other. It was well known that the first fishing sailboats to reach port got the best prices for their catches; the last ones to come home received the lowest. This is how racing started, and it soon became popular with both the local Beach Haven boat captains and wealthy sportsmen.

Whenever two sailboats are in proximity, there is great temptation to race each other. Dr. E.H. Williams of Beach Haven was the first man to have a racing catboat in Little Egg Harbor Bay. *Sayonara* was designed and built by the renowned naval architect Nathaniel Herreshoff at his boatworks in Bristol, Rhode Island. She was contracted in 1891, and launched on May 9, 1892, at a cost of $1,750. Constructed of wood, she was 29 feet long with a beam of 11 feet and a draft of 2 feet. This photograph depicts her sleek lines and fuller sail. Dr. Williams had a professional captain who participated regularly in races up and down Little Egg Harbor and Barnegat Bays. *Sayonara* competed yearly in the Toms River Challenge Cup that was started by the Toms River Yacht Club in 1871 for all catboats from the southern end of Long Beach Island to Mansquan Inlet. Captains and crew members enjoyed this yearly competition, which included the older working catboats and the newer racing type. Friendly betting, camaraderie, and high-spirited racing were all part of the Toms River Challenge Cup.

This small catboat has a full sail and is moving along at a fast pace. This racing catboat has only the skipper aboard. The sail is perfectly rigged except for a slight constriction with the lazy jacks on both sides of the sail. Lazy jacks caught the sail when it was dropped so it could be easily furled. Robert Fry Engle took this shot from a boat slightly ahead.

The racing yacht *Sayonara* was made of wood with lead ballast.

This image shows two catboats sailing side by side. The one to the left has lowered its gaff, leaving more air in the sail (good for a calm day), while the boat to the right has its gaff higher, with the thinking that it will catch more air because of its height. Robert Fry Engle took hundreds of photographs of catboats, capturing their classic beauty as they sailed.

Eight

HUNTING AND FISHING IN BEACH HAVEN

Situated in the sand behind the Baldwin Hotel, the Corinthian Yacht Club was originally called the Beach Haven Gun Club. Most notable was the large fireplace into which guns, shells, pipes, and all sorts of memorabilia were pushed in the cement during construction in 1904. Charles Beck was president when the club was dissolved, and the members formed the Little Egg Harbor Yacht Club.

CORINTHIAN YACHT & GUN CLUB, BEACH HAVEN, N. J.

Guide to
Game Fishing
at . . .

BEACH HAVEN

N E W   J E R S E Y

Compliments of . . .
B E A C H   H A V E N   Y A C H T   C L U B

Exclusive private clubs for specific activities were formed in Beach Haven. In 1907, the Corinthian Yacht and Gun Club was formed after the Beach Haven Gun Club failed to draw enough interest. James Baird and Charles Beck were charter members. This photograph shows the building just completed, with a gas lamp out front, which was lit every evening and extinguished in the morning. Gas lighting came to Beach Haven in 1901.

Beach Haven was proclaimed the "Fishing Capital of the World" and was proud of the title. The hub was the Beach Haven Yacht Club, where seasoned, proud captains took people out fishing in the bay and ocean. Each boat charged per person, thus the term "head boat."

Surf fishing was popularized by Margaret and Edward Gerhard, who had a bait and tackle and notions store on Beach Avenue in North Beach Haven. It is said that the Gerhards walked into the surf in their wool bathing suits and threw out lines. This act sparked the island's surf fishing enthusiasm, which continues today with many tournaments.

By the 1930s, bay fishing was a popular sport. All ages participated; no experience was needed. Fish such as croakers, blowfish, weakfish, bluefish, kingfish, and stripers were always found in the Beach Haven waters. They all made for a good dinner.

FISHING. BEACH HAVEN, N. J.

SURF-CASTING OFF SHORE
There are plenty of big ones to be caught right off the beach.

The Beach Haven Fishing Pier was a popular spot to drop a line or just socialize. Constructed in 1924 by contractor and icehouse owner Earl King, it was located at Berkeley Avenue and could be accessed from the Beach Haven boardwalk. It washed away with the boardwalk in the 1944 hurricane, leaving one lone piling standing until its removal in January 2018.

During the first years, the Beach Haven Fishing Pier was free for all fishermen. However, in 1927, the town put up a gate and charged 50¢ per day to use the facility, which ran 200 feet out into the ocean. There were many types of fish caught, and ducks were shot from the pier in the winter.

Unloading Fishing Boats on Long Beach Island, N. J.

Pound fishing took place on Long Beach Island from the late 1800s through World War II. A pound was a net trap a half mile out in the ocean held up by tall hickory poles designed to catch a variety of fish moving up or down the coast. Sturdy wooden pound boats brought fish onto the beach each morning.

POUND FISHERIES LONG BEACH, N.J.

Most pound fishermen were of Norwegian heritage and were big, strong, hardworking men. It took a half-dozen men to maneuver a pound boat into the surf and out to the pound, fill it with fish, and return. Horses—and later, tractors—pulled the pound boats up to the top of the beach.

SURF-CASTING IN THE BREAKERS

This postcard is titled *Surf-Casting in the Breakers*. Two young ladies, looking splendid in their daring, dark-colored, one-piece wool bathing suits, pose for a picture taken in the late 1920s. At this time, bathing costume regulations were eased a bit from ones that covered most of women's bodies, either longer skirts or bloomers underneath, to the less restrictive tank types. It is doubtful these girls ever seriously surf fished; their laughs, colorful head scarves, and awkwardness in handling the rods tell the story. During the 1930s, men began to shed their regulation tops and could swim with just trunks. The two largest hotels, the Engleside and Baldwin, still required guests to change from day clothes to bathing suits and back again in their bathhouses. Attendants for the men's and ladies' bathhouses rinsed and dried their wool suits, hanging them on the line for the next day's usage. There was a great fear of sand clogging the old pipes.

Channel Bass, with rod and reel. Surf at Beach Haven, N. J.

Surf fishing had become popular ever since Charles and Margaret Gerhard popularized the new sport. According to George Somerville's *The Lure of Long Beach*, "Beach Haven stood aghast one summer morning in 1907 to see Mr. and Mrs. Gerhard attired in bathing suits and armed with rods and reels, wade out into the surf and cast. But, when, after a hard thirty-minute fight, a huge twenty-pound channel bass (or drumfish) was brought ashore by Mrs. Gerhard, Beach Haven woke up to the possibility of its surf fishing." The gentleman in this image, taken two decades later in front of the Engleside Hotel, has dressed the part with high boots, an inappropriate jacket that was soon wet, pith helmet, and long wooden pipe in his mouth. He could brag about his own channel bass, caught in the ocean after casting his line as far out in the breakers as he could. This postcard is titled *Channel bass, with rod and reel. Surf at Beach Haven, NJ.*

THE FLEET AT THE DOCK AFTER A SUCCESSFUL DAY ON THE DEEP

By 1910, owners of boats in the large catboat fleet realized motors would work on their sailboats. Old Ford motors were placed in the centers of the boats and the masts were cut off to about a foot above the deck. Greater mobility was now possible for these sailboats after the conversion, allowing them to get to the fishing grounds quickly.

Robert Fry Engle took this photograph just after daybreak when the birds would usually fly overhead. Waiting for his prey, a lone hunter takes aim from his gunning box. Engle was no doubt part of a group of hunters in the marshy islands.

A garvey sits tied to a dock while a few eager fishermen prepare their lines. Fishing was foremost in popularity in Beach Haven for a half century and was made famous in newspapers and magazines. It attracted famous outdoorsmen, such as Van Campen Heilner, who wrote about saltwater fishing.

A proud young man shows off his prize red drum. Fishing was enjoyed in both the bay and ocean off Beach Haven. The sport enhanced business for hotels, boardinghouses, and restaurants as people came from Philadelphia and New York just to fish.

The Tueckmantels bought the Acme Hotel and Restaurant in 1925. It was a popular place for fishermen and hunters and close to the charter boats for fishing and hunting guides. It was said to be a colorful place for partygoers. They later owned Gus and Whiteys at Engleside and West Avenues, which today is Tucker's Restaurant.

Herman Joorman Jr. was born in 1904 in Burma. He was a lifeguard at the Engleside Hotel where he met his wife, Mary Elizabeth "Polly" Sumner. Together, they ran a small boat rental business and sold bait for years, spending their winters in Florida. Their boats look like small garveys with low-powered engines.

Polly and Herman Joorman worked Polly's Dock for decades. It became synonymous with hard work, family, and camaraderie. Their rental boats had kerosene lanterns for night fishing. The clientele was mainly from Philadelphia. Mink and otters were sometimes tame, sitting on the dock along with seagulls and egrets.

Along with selling bait, Polly's Dock rented small motorized boats by the hour for crabbing, fishing, and clamming. It was always full of local characters and visitors. Polly's Dock remains active today, the dock itself virtually unchanged, on West Avenue between Parker's Garage and Oyster Saloon to the north and newly constructed condos to the south.

Jim Priestley owned Priestley's Marina. In this 1940s photograph, these fishermen are proud of their catches, which range from small tuna to a white marlin. No doubt they had been on one of the Priestley's Marina charter boats for the day. In the winters, Jim Priestley made cedar sailing sneakboxes for children to race.

The Beach Haven Yacht Club hosted a number of fishing tournaments. Capt. Jack Whitaker (left) and crew of the *Miss Kensington* pose for a picture with their catch at the Beach Haven Yacht Club, located between Centre Street and Engleside Avenue. The *Miss Kensington* was a high-end sportfishing boat from the Atlantic City State Marina. It was owned by the Kensington Furniture Company located on Tilton Road in Northfield.

Sportsmen came to Beach Haven to fish with the expert captains who could be hired to take them out in the ocean to catch tuna. These men pose with four tuna hanging from a rack at the weigh station at the Beach Haven Yacht Club. This was a great catch for the day.

BIG-GAME TUNA — THE "WARHORSE OF THE ATLANTIC"

Here is the evidence of some big fellows who give the sportsman many a thrill. Many catches like the above are brought in every season, and while these range in weight up to 150 pounds, some have been caught in our pound nets weighing as high as 1000 pounds, showing there is no limit to the size that may be taken.

THE GAMEY MARLIN SWORDFISH

Only at Beach Haven can this warrior of the sea be persuaded to come aboard at the end of a line

This photograph is titled *The Gamey Marlin Swordfish*. The white marlin was one of the many fish caught in the ocean from aboard professional charter boats that took their clienteles out for larger fish. These two fishermen are proud of their catch. Beach Haven guides were some of the first in New Jersey to take fishermen out in the ocean for a day of fishing.

107

Public Deep Sea Fishing Fleet

A Good Catch on Long Beach Island, N. J.

The Beach Haven bayfront was filled with charter fishing boats during the 1920s and 1930s. The Acme Hotel and Restaurant is on the left side of this picture; to the right is the public dock where fishing captains had steady charters. Many of these captains took their boats and skills to Florida for the winter.

Local baymen became excellent charter boat captains who could almost guarantee a good catch such as these weakfish. Fishing continued to evolve as techniques changed and captains became more proficient. By the 1950s, owning their own boats was becoming a way of life for fishermen.

Robert Fry Engle studied and was trained to be a professional photographer before his father called him back to New Jersey to run the Engleside Hotel. As a result, some of his photographs seem posed. Both father and son also enjoyed fishing, as seen here with a catch of weakfish laid out to look appealing.

This Robert Fry Engle photograph is a posed collection of recently shot birds lying on a porch. These are snipe, a type of marsh bird. Both Robert Barclay Engle and his son Robert Fry Engle were avid hunters. They joined many hunting parties at Charles Beck's "farm."

Winter put a stop to fishing, except for the diehards who drilled holes in the ice for eels. The bay used to freeze on a regular basis. Ice and snow, along with the tidal flow, caused pilings to be pulled out of the bay mud. In the background is the Beach Haven Yacht Club in its later years, when a popular dining room was added.

POLLY'S DOCK
(KELLY'S DOCK PRIOR TO 1943)

An image of a bad winter at Polly's Dock shows pilings and docks along the bayfront that have been damaged by ice and changing tides. The pilings were lifted as the ice frozen to them rose with the tide. They would be repaired in the spring before business began.

Nine

BEACH HAVEN
FIRST RESPONDERS

Founded April 28, 1883, the Beach Haven Volunteer Fire Company No. 1 was established and chartered through the Tuckerton and Long Beach Island Land Association. This photograph, taken shortly after its establishment, shows a ladder cart and two hand-drawn hose carts used by its volunteers. As the oldest fire company in Ocean County, it was created followed a devastating fire that destroyed one of the borough's grand hotels, the Parry House.

THE FIRE HOUSE.   BEACH HAVEN, N. J.

Taken by Jacob Britz, this photograph shows a young boy looking to the south; the firehouse and borough hall are on the left and the Beach Haven House, at Centre Street and Bay Avenue, is shown at right. The Beach Haven Volunteer Fire Company No. 1 originally served the entire island.

From 1883 to 1915, the Beach Haven Volunteer Fire Company No. 1 was located next to the borough's water tower at Engleside and Bay Avenues. Founding members were Samuel Cowperthwaite, John Marshall, James Sprague, Henry Ireland, William Butler, Charles Cox, Hiram Lamson, George Dayton, John Fox, and George Walker. In 1933, its massive bell tower was removed and a siren was installed on the borough's water tank.

Among the volunteer firefighters shown in this photograph, Lou Rossell can be seen in the first row, second from the right; Capt. Carol Stratton, seen first row, fourth from the right, served on the Beach Haven Borough Council and was fire chief for 15 years. In 1914, the first Turkey Dinner Fundraiser was held at the Green Gables Inn on Centre Street to raise funds for the company's operation.

Capt. Carol Stratton and Lou Rossell pose for a photograph in front of the Beach Haven Fire House. Stratton, owner of Stratton Freight, died on January 14, 1938, at the age of 51, leaving behind a wife and four young children. Firefighting was hard work, and it has been noted that his services as a volunteer firefighter may have contributed to the heart attack that took his life.

Local newspapers, including the *Beachcomber*, owned by Margaret Buchholz, often paid tribute to the importance of local volunteer fire service and the roles of its members in saving lives and property. Fundraising events, including turkey dinners, carnivals, and donkey baseball, drew the attendance of residents throughout the island and nearby mainland communities.

In addition to serving the residents and visitors of Beach Haven, the Beach Haven Volunteer Fire Company No. 1 also provided service to the residents of Long Beach Township, from Eighty-Fifth Street to the southernmost tip of Holgate, after other municipalities established their own companies.

While filling the tanks at the Esso gas station at Fifth and Bay Avenue, a fuel truck caught fire on July 1, 1958, requiring the response of all available volunteers. Just two years after this, on September 24, 1960, the Baldwin Hotel caught fire, requiring the assistance of over 20 fire companies from throughout Ocean and Atlantic Counties.

This image depicts the efforts of the Beach Haven Volunteer Fire Company No. 1 volunteers to contain this inferno and protect the homes and businesses in its vicinity. During all major structural fires, mutual aid is often called upon to minimize damages and assist in the containment of the fire. Members of the borough's volunteer fire aid squad are called to provide additional support for the firefighters.

EXPLOSION - FIFTH STREET GAS STATION

Throughout the 1920s and 1930s, fundraisers were held to raise much-needed funds for the purchase of equipment; carnivals, turkey dinners, bingo games, car raffles, and moonlight sails from the Little Egg Harbor Yacht Club and Beach Haven Yacht Club were among the events held for this purpose.

In November 1940, the Beach Haven Volunteer Fire Company No. 1 sponsored the establishment of the Beach Haven First Aid Squad. Although the Memorial Ambulance Commission of Beach Haven was formed in 1937, incorporation of the Beach Haven First Aid Squad was not completed until 1941.

Among the early ambulances purchased by the Beach Haven First Aid Squad were a 1941 Cadillac Silver Knightstown, 1947 Cadillac Meteor, 1951 DeSoto Conversion, 1954 Cadillac Miller, 1958 Pontiac National, eight Cadillac S&S models (a 1956, three 1962s, a 1965, two 1967s, and a 1969), two Cadillac Miller Meteors (1970 and 1971), and a 1973 Cadillac Superior.

The vehicles shown here are a 1947 Cadillac Meteor (left) and a 1941 Cadillac Knightstown. In addition to their duties as emergency medical technicians (EMTs) and drivers, members of the Beach Haven First Aid Squad are responsible for the maintenance of its fleet of ambulances, replenishment of medical supplies, and the upkeep of its headquarters.

Volunteers of the Beach Haven First Aid Squad, including Walt Osborn, third from left, and Charlie Pinnix, second from right, provided an invaluable service to the visitors and residents of Beach Haven, Long Beach Township, and Ship Bottom. Not unlike the mutual-aid policies of the Beach Haven Volunteer Fire Company No. 1, the borough's volunteer first-aid squad was often called upon to assist on calls outside its regular coverage area.

As the need to replace older vehicles arose, this 1954 Cadillac Miller, 1947 Cadillac Meteor, and 1951 DeSoto Conversion Transport vehicle were put into service to cover the emergency medical calls within Beach Haven First Aid Squad's coverage area. The operation of these emergency vehicles under harsh conditions—not to mention frequent coastal flooding—shortened the lifespan of many of them, requiring frequent replacement.

This 1954 Cadillac Miller is shown outside the ambulance bay of the Beach Haven First Aid Squad's first home at Amber Street. A dedication ceremony was held in the summer of 1950. In its constitution and bylaws, the squad's purpose shall be "to answer calls of an emergency nature, and operate emergency ambulance service for the communities of Beach Haven, Long Beach Township, and Ship Bottom, New Jersey."

The dedicated volunteers shown here, from left to right and identified only by their last names, are Parker, Cranmer, Fackler, unidentified, Ruggerio, Cranmer, and Moffett. Membership in the Beach Haven Volunteer First Aid Squad was classified as follows: Active, Inactive, Probationary, Affiliated, and Honorary. While some members held the necessary medical certificates to provide patient care, others opted to volunteer as drivers with basic lifesaving skills.

This 1962 Cadillac/S&S was one of three of the same units operating from the Beach Haven Headquarters; the squad's coverage area included Beach Haven, Ship Bottom, and Long Beach Township north to the southern boundary of Surf City. The Ship Bottom division, located at the corner of Twentieth Street and Central Avenue in Ship Bottom, was later established in 1976 as a secondary headquarters to accommodate the growing fleet and volume of calls.

The members shown in this photograph, wearing official first-aid squad uniforms required at the time, are, from left to right, ? Cranmer, George Wiltshire, Warren Gifford, Evelyn Cranmer, unidentified, and George Binet. At one time, *All My Children* actor Craig Austin (whose real name was Craig Hoffmeyer) volunteered as an EMT during the summer months while on vacation from filming.

Posing for the dedication of the first Beach Haven First Aid Squad headquarters on Amber Street in 1950, from left to right, are Les Parker, Capt., Ernest Cramer, Charles Brewer, Walt Osborn, Stan Scull, Paul Green, Harry Marshall, Robert Fritsch, Otto Meyer, Tilton Mathis, Hillard Grant, Rod Conor, Charley Pinnix, Robert Osborn, James Hart, Howard King, and Charles Lamb.

Posing in front of the newly constructed Engleside Avenue headquarters of the Beach Haven First Aid Squad, dedicated November 13, 1960, squad members include Lester Parker, first row, second from left; Phyllis Gee, first row, fifth from left; Betty Priestly, first row, sixth from left; and Skip and Carol Rossell, second row behind Gee.

Beach Haven Volunteer First Aid Squad's coverage area includes 10 of the 18 miles of Long Beach Island, from Ship Bottom to Holgate. Motor vehicle accidents account for many of the calls for service, as shown on this photograph taken on the causeway that connects the mainland to the island.

Overturned vehicles were not an uncommon site when local merrymakers overimbibed at one of the town's local establishments; the Acme Hotel on Dock Road was a favorite of many, especially during the days of Prohibition, straining the resources of the squad. Many of these calls required the collective assistance of the borough's police department, fire company, and first-aid squad.

Dedicated in November 1960, the second home of the Beach Haven Volunteer First Aid Squad was situated on Engleside Avenue, facing the entrance to the Beach Haven Police Department. This building served the needs of emergency medical personnel until 1997, when it was razed to make way for a larger facility.

As the year-round and seasonal population of Long Beach Island continued to increase, the need for emergency medical services also increased; additional ambulances and equipment needed to stock these vehicles necessitated the expansion of the Beach Haven headquarters. This photograph shows the current building, completed in 1998, and several of its fleet of emergency vehicles. When the Ship Bottom division was established, these ambulances were equally distributed to both so that calls could be answered from either building, contingent on the proximity of the call.

**CHRIS SPRAGUE
WITH BEACH HAVEN POLICE CAR**

Chris Sprague, an officer—and later, chief—of the Beach Haven Police Department, poses in front of an early model of his department's patrol car. Crime consisted mostly of minor infractions and rarely necessitated the incarceration of unsavory characters. Members of the Sprague family can be found throughout the history of Beach Haven and are among the earliest of the town's residents.

Officer Chris Sprague of the Beach Haven Police Department, on Bay Avenue, is appropriately outfitted with the uniform of the day. Sprague was also known as an avid decoy carver, and his decoys are highly prized among collectors. Many of the town's police officers also worked as volunteers for the fire department and first-aid squad during their off-duty hours. This practice continues today.

Beach Haven's finest are pictured in this 1977 photograph. From left to right are Mike Kassardy, Hugh Sprague, Bill Coates, Jay Vigdor, John Horvath, Ed Meyers, Chief Arno Kohler, Ernie Senior, Chick Lamson, Dave Brown, John Lipko, Bill Martin, and John Cathcart. Soon after this photograph was taken, Chief Kohler died at the age of 45. His son Kevin Kohler filled his shoes as chief from 2008 to 2017. Today's Police Department of the Borough of Beach Haven is under the jurisdiction and control of the borough manager. Pursuant to the borough code, "The Police Department shall consist of not more than ten (10) patrol officers, four (4) Sergeants, two (2) Lieutenants, one (1) Captain, and one (1) Chief, and other members and personnel who shall, from time to time, be deemed to be necessary for the preservation of peace and good order within the Borough of Beach Haven and as the Borough Manager may deem necessary and hereinafter appoint." In January 2018, Beach Haven's police department came under the command of Chief James Markoski.

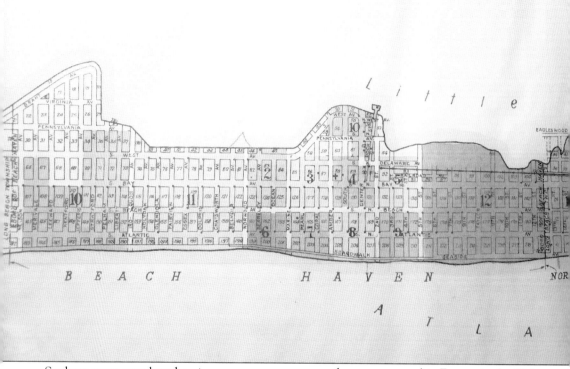

Sanborn maps were based on insurance company maps that were created in Europe in the 18th century and spread to the United States in the mid-19th century. Daniel Alfred Sanborn was a civil engineer and surveyor and owner of D. Sanborn National Insurance Diagram Bureau in New York. Once used to assess fire insurance liability, these maps today are invaluable to historians. They include 12,000 US towns and cities, and were bound into area books, with changes monitored on little pieces of paper designed to be pasted into the volumes. Details include size-scaled dwellings complete with outbuildings, location of windows and doors, building usage, and building materials. House numbers were used for homes, churches, and schools; also included was the town population, economy, and fire insurance information such as location of fire hydrants, gas, and water mains. The New Jersey Maritime Museum owns two original books of Beach Haven and some of the island. Researchers, historians, and genealogists study the Sanborn maps to provide information on Beach Haven's old homes. They are available to visitors at the New Jersey Maritime Museum.

About the New Jersey Maritime Museum

The New Jersey Maritime Museum is the culmination of a lifetime of dedication to the subject by Deborah Whitcraft. While in her teens, she became a certified scuba diver whose curiosity about local shipwrecks led to over 40 years of research. On July 3, 2007, her ambition was fulfilled when the museum opened its doors to the public. Upon its completion, the New Jersey Maritime Museum was turned over to the Museum of New Jersey Maritime History Inc., a registered 501(c)(3) nonprofit organization.

When the museum opened, almost all of its contents were from Whitcraft's personal collection. Since then, due to the generosity of the diving community and many private citizens, the collection and exhibits have grown at an astonishing rate. From the New Jersey shipwreck files that encompass nearly 5,000 known maritime disasters to its collection of artifacts recovered from these wrecks, there is something to interest visitors of all ages. There are nearly 400 notebooks covering subjects from shipwrecks, coastal towns and history, marine industries, and genealogy. Its diverse collection has made the museum an invaluable resource for researchers and students alike. With determination to preserve this important part of history, the museum's motto is "If it's not shared, it has no value."

Visitors to the museum will find many exhibits covering topics from the US Life-Saving Service and Coast Guard, Atlantic City, diving, navigation, and shipbuilding to displays devoted to individual shipwrecks. There is an entire room devoted to the 1934 *Morro Castle* disaster, considered by many to be New Jersey's own *Titanic*. This room contains what is, without doubt, the largest collection of *Morro Castle* memorabilia in existence. The museum also houses a rare book library that is available for on-site research and a public lending library for the use of its members. Throughout the building, many videos and slide shows covering a variety of maritime related subjects are available for viewing.

From the many programs available to the public, ranging from summer children's activities to monthly guest presentations, the New Jersey Maritime Museum has become a must-see attraction for those who wish to learn more about New Jersey's rich maritime history. It is located at 528 Dock Road in Beach Haven. Call 609-492-0202 or visit www.NJMM.org.

DISCOVER THOUSANDS OF LOCAL HISTORY BOOKS
FEATURING MILLIONS OF VINTAGE IMAGES

Arcadia Publishing, the leading local history publisher in the United States, is committed to making history accessible and meaningful through publishing books that celebrate and preserve the heritage of America's people and places.

Find more books like this at
www.arcadiapublishing.com

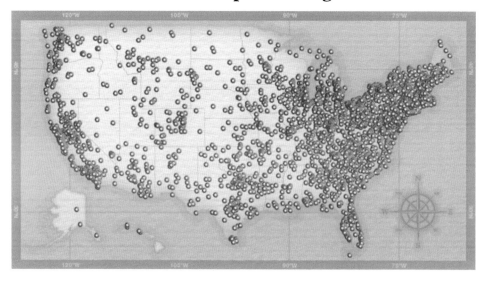

Search for your hometown history, your old stomping grounds, and even your favorite sports team.